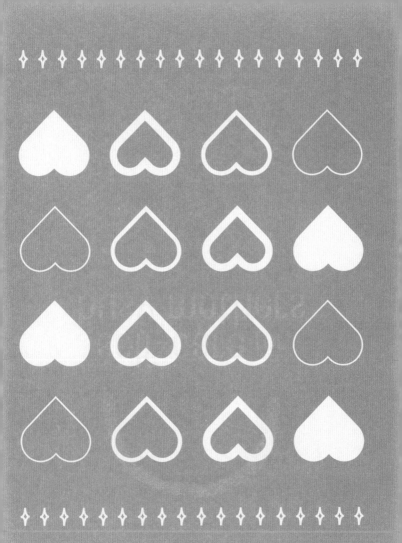

self-care for busy mothers

simple steps to find peace and balance

sarah rudell beach

CICO BOOKS
LONDON NEW YORK

For Abby and Liam
I love you to the moon and back, and I love being your mom.

Published in 2023 by CICO Books
An imprint of Ryland Peters & Small Ltd
20–21 Jockey's Fields   341 E 116th St
London WC1R 4BW   New York, NY 10029

www.rylandpeters.com

10 9 8 7 6 5 4 3 2 1

Abridged from *Mindful Moments for Busy Mothers,* first published in 2018

Text © Sarah Rudell Beach 2023
Design and illustration © CICO Books 2023

A CIP catalog record for this book is available from the
Library of Congress and the British Library.

ISBN: 978-1-80065-191-3

Printed in China

Editor: Slav Todorov
Senior designer: Emily Breen

Commissioning editor: Kristine Pidkameny
Senior commissioning editor: Carmel Edmonds
Art director: Sally Powell
Creative director: Leslie Harrington
Head of production: Patricia Harrington
Publishing manager: Penny Craig

CONTENTS

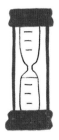

INTRODUCTION

As a mother, you've heard the advice about putting on your own oxygen mask before assisting your children and how you can't pour from an empty cup. You hear all these maxims because they're true. The problem is that a lot of the self-care advice out there for mothers focuses on "quick fixes," or you're told to "just treat yourself" to a massage and a pedicure once in a while.

But as a busy mother, you need something that goes deeper. You need something that works on a soul level, a practice that can be woven into your days, and transforms how you approach all the parts of your life, including motherhood.

That's where mindfulness comes in. Mindfulness seems to be everywhere now, and you probably already know that being present and peaceful would be really good for your emotional health (hey, you're reading this book, after all!) But a lot of the time, despite your best intentions to bring a calm and compassionate awareness to the act of mothering, you often do the opposite: you end up overreacting, yelling, issuing threats, stressing out, and feeling defeated and depleted.

I know this because I've been there. I came to the practice of mindfulness over a decade ago, as a new mother struggling with postpartum depression. I had desperately wanted to be a mother, and was completely in love with my daughter, but I was miserable.

But I wanted to get better, so I gave mindfulness a try. I sat down on a pillow on my bedroom floor and closed my eyes. It felt a little weird, but I stayed on that pillow, allowing my body to soften as I tried to release all the holding and bracing I had been doing for so many years. I found that as my body became a bit more still and relaxed, so did my mind.

Mindfulness gave me such a gift that I began to pursue an entirely new career direction, as I transitioned from being a high school history teacher to becoming a full-time mindfulness instructor. I now spend my days teaching mindfulness to mothers, children, teachers, students, and now, YOU.

what is mindfulness and why do mothers need it?

Neuroscientist Rick Hanson has recently suggested that mothers in the developed world are suffering from what he calls Depleted Mom Syndrome. Mothers still carry the work of the so-called "second shift," are sleep- and exercise-deprived, and, according to Hanson, we suffer from "guilt, anxiety, conflicting role expectations … mood swings, irritability, [and] hopelessness."

The mothers I work with are overwhelmed, stressed out, distracted, busy, overscheduled, and rushing through their days, with a sense that they are missing out on their own lives. Hanson and other psychologists agree: what mothers need is self-care, emotional awareness and acceptance, and greater presence and wellbeing. Mindfulness is the most powerful tool I know of for helping mothers do all of that.

Mindfulness helps us regulate our emotional responses and soothe our overtaxed nervous systems. It allows us to find a place of peace and stability within our own bodies, so we can experience nourishing self-care when and where we need it, not just at the spa. Mindfulness helps us keep our cool when our children are fired up, and, I can tell you from my own personal experience, keeps us from losing our … ahem, stuff every day.

what it looks like when mothers practice mindfulness

Let's break down that definition of mindfulness:

PURPOSEFUL AWARENESS OF THE PRESENT MOMENT

Sometimes we're paying attention, but not on purpose. It's the honk of another car, or a child yelling for you the tenth time that day that jolts us out of our distraction. Mindfulness is paying attention on purpose. Mindfulness is an intentional awareness of the sensations, thoughts, feelings, and experiences of the present moment.

We spend a lot of our time thinking about the past or planning for the future. When we are mindful, we are paying attention to our present moment experience. For example, if you serve dinner and your child immediately responds with, "But I hate chicken," you would pay attention to your body's response—your racing pulse, your clenched jaw, the anger rising in your chest. You wouldn't stop all those responses, you would simply become aware of them. But instead of letting that anger lead to a long-winded speech about your continuous acts of sacrifice for your family, mindfulness would help you …

ACCEPT WHAT IS HAPPENING RIGHT NOW, WITH CURIOSITY AND WITHOUT JUDGMENT

You would allow the present moment to be what it is … because it's already here and happening.

You wouldn't have to like the present moment—you can find it pretty unpleasant to cook your famous chicken parmesan only to have your child complain about it—but you wouldn't fight that it's actually happening. Instead, you'd accept it without judgment, and get curious: Why is my child getting upset? Did something happen today? Why am I getting so upset about the fact that she's getting upset? Did something happen today? When I first started practicing mindfulness, I thought not judging things meant I had to like everything in every moment and think that everything that happened was amazing and wonderful.

WHAT IS MINDFULNESS?

Mindfulness is purposeful awareness of the present moment. With mindfulness, we accept what is happening right now, with curiosity and without judgment. Mindfulness means we know what we are thinking when we are thinking it, and what we are feeling when we're feeling it. It gives us the ability to pause, and to respond skillfully to challenges, instead of reacting based on our unconscious habits. Mindfulness brings us into the only moment we have—now—and allows us to see the goodness (or even just the okayness) that is present even in the most ordinary of experiences.

✧ ✧

The butterflies and rainbows and whining and tantrums and potty-training—they're all beautiful! I'm so Zen!

Mindfulness is about being with the entire range of our human experience, whether it is pleasant or unpleasant. So once you've noticed what's happening, gotten curious about it, and accepted it without judgment, you would …

PAUSE AND RESPOND SKILLFULLY, INSTEAD OF REACTING BASED ON YOUR UNCONSCIOUS HABITS

You would pause and breathe and instead of falling into your default mode (an epic sermon about your mama-martyrdom), you would lovingly remind your child of the last time she ate this meal and how much she enjoyed it. Or you might offer her the choice of what will be for dinner tomorrow night. Or you might do something else that's skillful and doesn't make the situation worse.

SO HOW CAN YOU LEARN TO DO THIS?

One of the most important things about mindfulness is that it is a practice. It's something we must cultivate—we can't just read a book, decide to appreciate mindfulness and peacefulness and attentiveness from now on, and expect things to change, any more than we can read a book about exercise, decide to appreciate sweat and movement, and expect to be more fit.

We have to practice. Mindfulness is like a muscle, something that will grow stronger the more we use it. The more we practice pausing, the better we will get at it. The more we practice being fully present with our breath, the better we will get at being fully present with our children. The more aware we become of the patterns of our thoughts, the less we'll be driven by them, and we'll be able to change some of our reactive habits that aren't serving us very well. And, according to the research, we'll experience less stress and greater joy. All of these things can help you enjoy motherhood more, and help you be the mother you want to be. I like to think of our work as that of mindful motherhood, not mindful parenting.

AND HOW DO YOU FIND THE TIME?

When you're really busy, you might think taking five minutes to meditate just isn't worth it, because then you'll be even more behind schedule. But we often "earn back" the time we spend in mindfulness practice.

A famous Zen saying tells us that if we don't have one hour for meditation in our day, then we need at least two. I don't know any mother that has two hours for daily meditation, but I'm pretty sure you have five minutes! (And if you don't have five, you probably need ten!) Although it's important to create time for your mindfulness practice in your day, it's also important to not make mindfulness just another item on your To-Do list, a chore that must be completed. Mindfulness should be a "get to," not a "have to." Think of ways that you can ritualize your practice—maybe lighting a candle or listening to soothing music—so that your time feels special and set apart from the rest of your day. Allow your time for mindfulness to be a gift you give yourself.

how to use this book

This book is intended to provide both guidance and inspiration for your mindfulness practice. You'll discover lots of different ways to bring mindfulness into your busy-mama days. Think of this book as a menu, not an all-you-can-eat buffet.

Sample the exercises that appeal to you, experiment with them in the laboratory of your own life, and see what works for you. If a particular practice brings you some ease and comfort, you can come back for seconds.

a few notes about the meditations:

1. Some meditations begin with an instruction to "Close your eyes…" Read the meditation a few times, and then close your eyes and practice. You could also have someone read them to you, or you could dictate them into your phone and use the recording to practice.

2. This is a book about mindfulness and meditation. What's the difference? Mindfulness is a broad term, referring to our ability to attend to the present moment no matter what we are doing. It is something we can cultivate throughout our day, even as we engage in other activities. When I use the word "meditation," I am referring to the formal practice in which we sit (or lie) down, close our eyes, and deliberately bring our attention to a particular aspect of our experience (the breath, for example).

3. If you fall asleep during your meditation time, that's okay. It's just a nap. And if you fell asleep that quickly, you probably needed a nap far more than you needed meditation.
You can do things like adjusting your posture and choosing a time of day to practice when you'll be most alert, but it's also totally fine to be so present with your sleepiness that you fall asleep.

4. You may think you are "bad" at mindfulness and meditation because your mind wanders a lot and keeps doing all this thinking when you're trying to be mindful. But when you notice that your mind has wandered away from the present moment, that's actually great news! It means you are becoming more aware of the activity of your mind—it wandered, and you noticed. That means you're absolutely doing it right.

CHAPTER 1

BEGIN

MINDFULNESS PRACTICES

Mornings offer a bewildering array of experiences. One morning you may be able to linger in the sweetness and stillness of the first few moments of a day when the world has not yet demanded much of you. And then on other days the morning is a chaotic blur of being woken early (after a night full of interruptions), dragging older kids out of bed, getting breakfasts and backpacks ready, ushering everyone out the door, and getting yourself to work on time. Mornings can be a great time to practice mindfulness, however, because no matter what the day has in store for you, you can begin with a few moments of mindful reflection that prepare you to meet the new day with intention and presence.

scan your body

Close your eyes, and as you breathe, gently scan your body. See if you can identify somewhere in your body that feels pleasant, perhaps a sense of relaxation in the face, or warmth in the hands. Spend some time with this sensation. How do you know it is pleasant? What is pleasant about it? How does it feel to spend time focusing on a part of the body that feels good?

Then do the same thing with an unpleasant sensation: what is it, how do you know it's unpleasant, and what happens when you bring awareness to it? There's no "right" or "wrong" way to do this meditation, but you might notice that 1) you have some choice in where you place your attention, and 2) what you pay attention to can impact your present moment experience.

keep an open mind

Try to approach your practice without any preconceived ideas of how it's supposed to look or feel or be. You may find that your practice is relaxing, but that isn't the "goal." One day it might be relaxing. The next day it might be boring. And then the next day you just feel hungry and your back hurts. And then the day after that, you love it. Just notice whatever is happening when you practice—if you hate it, notice that you're hating it. If you are tense and irritated, notice that you are tense and irritated. If you think you are really bad at mindfulness, notice that you are thinking you are bad at mindfulness!

find the roots of the tree

We often refer to our minds as "monkey minds," because they jump from thought to thought as often as monkeys leap from branch to branch. As you practice mindfulness, you'll start to get familiar with the branches your monkey mind likes to swing around on. You might notice the same thought patterns and worries appear again and again in meditation. Perhaps a thought keeps popping up because there's something you need to resolve. Noticing these repetitive thought patterns is the beginning of insight.

I WILL FOCUS ON WHAT I CAN CONTROL.

know that it's just this

Whatever you're doing, just do it, and know that you are doing it.
Mindfulness is knowing you're …

Just cleaning   Just cooking
•
Just driving   Just walking
•
Just rocking   Just coloring
•
Just playing   Just talking
•
Just eating   Just sitting
•
Just singing   Just reading

just being

know your default setting

We all have a set of default thoughts and behaviors that we tend to enact when we get frustrated or overwhelmed or angry—heavy sighing, loud yelling, quiet crying, self-critical thinking … With mindfulness, you can become more aware of these unthinking, knee-jerk reactions, and you can start to interrupt them with a moment of presence. Then you can respond with a wise choice, based on what's actually happening, instead of relying on ingrained habits that don't always serve you. Throughout your day, notice your default settings and reactions, and see if you can make these unconscious behaviors conscious.

"soften"

I think this is sometimes the only mantra we need. Soften. Release the tension in your neck, shoulders, jaw, forehead, hands, eyes, legs, chest, torso, your entire body. Release your resistance. Soften your heart, allowing it to feel expansive and open. Meet this moment with softness and ease, meet your child with softness and ease, meet your thoughts with softness and ease. Take a deep breath, and soften. Repeat the mantra "Soften."

"I am perfect as I am"

Mindfulness is not about self-improvement. In fact, the fundamental insight of mindfulness is that you already have everything you need, right now in this moment. Right now you can breathe, you can find the clarity to see things as they are, and you can cultivate the wisdom to respond skillfully to what is in front of you. Mindfulness practice is not about changing who you are or trying to be a "better mother"; it's about learning to trust yourself as you find new ways to meet the challenges that arise each day. Repeat the mantra "I Am Perfect as I Am."

notice your race car mind

It's totally okay when you notice you have not just a racing mind, but a race car mind: a mind that whips around the track at ridiculous speeds, and never seems to need refueling. Like that race car, your mind gets stuck on a track, revisiting the same terrain over and over again, instead of venturing somewhere new. When you notice your race car mind, see if you can get out of the driver's seat (because this vehicle will go on without you), and simply stand in the grass in the middle of the track. See if you can just watch the speeding car without being thrown about on hairpin turns, without your heart racing as fast as those wheels spin. See if you can be the observer of your thoughts, and not the driver.

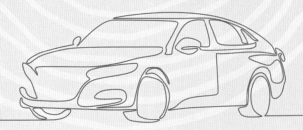

telescope your attention

Sometimes we must attend to one small part of our experience (such as reading a book or playing a game), and other times we need to zoom out and take in a great deal of information at once (when we're driving, for example). You can play with this telescoping of attention in your mindfulness practice. First, bring your attention to your breath and your body, and stay with that for a few minutes. Then see if you can expand your attention to your surroundings, noticing the air, sounds, and smells around you. Finally, try to expand your attention even further, extending out of the room and into the outside world, noticing any sounds or sense impressions, or simply imagine your awareness is expanding outward and upward toward the sky. Then you can play with bringing your attention back to the room, and finally to your breath.

enjoy a mental massage

Close your eyes, take a few deep breaths, and roll your shoulders back. Keeping your posture upright, allow yourself to release any tension in your neck and back. As you continue to focus on your breath, imagine someone gently placing her hands on the top of your head (you could even place your own hands there if you'd like). Imagine the feeling of warmth and soft pressure on your skull, and then pretend that her hands move to stroke your hair soothingly. Envision them lightly massaging your neck and shoulders, moving to exactly where you need relaxation. It might even help to think of a time you've had a pleasant massage or back rub, and remember the soothing sensations. Take a deep breath and savor this feeling of being nurtured and cared for.

listen to your body

Your emotions are almost always physical before they are conscious—there's a pit in your stomach, a trembling in your hands, or a new tension in your jaw that alerts you that something important is happening. Today, practice being aware of your body and the signals it sends. See if you can identify the unique markers of different emotions in your system, such as when you feel sad, angry, jealous, or happy. Cultivating this deep attunement with your body and its messages is a core component of emotional awareness.

I AM NOT MY THOUGHTS.

check your posture

There is an amazing relationship between how we hold our body, and how we feel. If we stand upright, with our shoulders back and our feet grounded on the earth, we feel confident and powerful. Try experimenting right now with standing up tall and proud, and notice how that feels. Then allow yourself to slouch, let your head droop forward, and draw your feet together as your body folds in on itself. Do you notice a difference? For today, practice checking in with your posture. Are you in a position that conveys alertness and confidence? Can you make subtle shifts in your body and see how that feels?

mindful moment

Breathe in and notice any tension in the body.
Breathe out and release the tension.
Breathe in and notice if judgments or
thoughts are present.
Breathe out and remember that
thoughts are just thoughts.
Breathe in and notice any emotions
that are present.
Breathe out and know that
this emotion is not you.
Breathe in and smile.
Breathe out and relax.

✧ ✧

I AM FOCUSED ON THIS TASK. I CAN DO JUST THIS.

practice coherent breathing

Some amazing scientists studied the "most relaxing" rate of breathing, and discovered that it's about five or six breaths per minute (compared to the average adult breathing rate of 12–15 breaths per minute). To practice coherent breathing, you can use a timer, or you can simply count in your head as you breathe in and out. To breathe six times per minute, count to five on the inhale, using all five seconds for your breath. It's important to make the in-breath last for the full five seconds, as opposed to taking a quick breath in and holding it. Then count to five on the exhale, slowly releasing the breath. Try it for two minutes and see how it feels. Do you feel more relaxed?

✦ ✦ ✦ ✦ ✦ ✦ ✦ ✦ ✦ ✦ ✦ ✦ ✦ ✦ ✦ ✦ ✦ ✦ ✦ ✦

CHAPTER 2

STARTING THE DAY

MORNING PRACTICES

Mornings offer a bewildering array of experiences. One morning you may be able to linger in the sweetness and stillness of the first few moments of a day when the world has not yet demanded much of you. And then on other days the morning is a chaotic blur of being woken early (after a night full of interruptions), dragging older kids out of bed, getting breakfasts and backpacks ready, ushering everyone out the door, and getting yourself to work on time. Mornings can be a great time to practice mindfulness, however, because no matter what the day has in store for you, you can begin with a few moments of mindful reflection that prepare you to meet the new day with intention and presence.

✦ ✦ ✦ ✦ ✦ ✦ ✦ ✦ ✦ ✦ ✦ ✦ ✦ ✦ ✦ ✦ ✦ ✦ ✦ ✦

the first moment of your day

If you can, don't rush yourself out of bed in the morning. A fussing child can wait for 30 seconds while you gently stretch. Feel the movement of your body, and consider your intention for the day. If you have a few more seconds, take a deep breath in, welcoming the strength and energy you will need for your day, and then breathe out while you imagine releasing worries and tension and anything else you don't need today.

early morning meditation

If you can, wake up 10 minutes (or more, if you'd like) earlier than your children. Sit upright on a cushion or your couch or your bed, and set a timer for 10 minutes. Close your eyes and bring your attention to your breath, and notice what it feels like to be awake when everyone else is sleeping. What sounds do you hear? Does the house feel different? Do you feel different? Morning meditations can sometimes be "easier" because the day has yet to intrude on your experience, and your busy, chattering mind may still be a bit sleepy. Experiment to discover what it feels like for you.

I WELCOME TODAY.

the first moment
with your child

In her book *Daring Greatly*, researcher Bren Brown recounts Toni Morrison's advice when speaking on "The Oprah Winfrey Show" about the first moments when we see our children each day. Morrison once said, "Let your face speak what's in your heart." Can you try to greet your children with a smile this morning? Can you begin the day on a positive note? I've noticed that sometimes my first words of the day to my children are, "Why are you up so early?" or "Hey, you don't have any pants on." I now try to make that first moment of the morning one of love and acceptance. See if you can first meet your child with a loving smile and a welcoming presence … and then you can worry about their pants.

"today I will practice curiosity"

Today I will look at the world with interest and curiosity. Instead of bringing my preconceived ideas and stories to the world, I will meet the world with a beginner's mind. I will be open to what unfolds, and approach my day with an eager inquisitiveness.

"today I will practice tenderness"

Today I will bring tenderness to all that I do. If today feels hard, I'll be soft and gentle with myself. When my child gets upset, I'll show compassion and warmth. I will practice tenderness with my voice, my body, and my thoughts.

morning body scan

In whatever posture is comfortable (lying down, sitting in a chair, nursing your baby on the couch), take a deep breath and bring your attention to your lower body (legs and feet). Just notice the sensations that are present, if any, and take a moment to set an intention for how you want to move in the world today—do you want to slow down, or will you need to be a bit speedier and more efficient today? Bring your awareness to your torso, noticing the sensations in your chest and belly. With your next breath, set an intention for how you want to feel today— energetic, restful, joyful, peaceful, or something else? Then gently bring your attention to your arms and hands, and set an intention for how you will be with your children today, imagining them in your embrace.

Finally, bring your awareness to your neck and face and head, and set an intention for how you will be present today. Take a few more deep breaths, and begin your day.

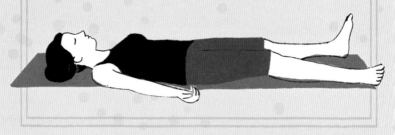

"today I will practice pride"

Today I will take pride in the things I do for my children, for myself, and for my world. I will honor myself for my hard work and all that I accomplish.

"today I will practice play"

Today I will allow myself to have fun. I will play with my kids and not worry about whether I'm being productive. I will seek joy and cultivate play.

"today I will practice quiet"

Today I will welcome quiet and stillness. I will not try to fill silences that do not need filling, and I will make time for moments of peace and calm.

"today I will practice authenticity"

Today I will be myself. Today I will give voice to my needs and my feelings, even if it's only to myself. I will not try to hide or cover up; I will be authentically me.

breakfast meditation

If you tend to skip breakfast, see if you can take a few moments to eat something healthy this morning, perhaps some yogurt or a piece of fruit, or peanut butter and banana on toast. If you can, try to really taste and enjoy the food, instead of eating on-the-go. Even if you only get three bites in silence, savor each one and allow eating breakfast to be a truly nourishing, if brief, experience.

TODAY I WILL BE PRESENT.

✦ ✧ ✦ ✧ ✦ ✧ ✦ ✧ ✦ ✧ ✦ ✧ ✦ ✧ ✦ ✧ ✦ ✧ ✦ ✧

CHAPTER 3

NURTURE
MINDFUL MOTHERHOOD

If being a mindful mother doesn't mean we're perfect, what does it mean? Well, it simply means we apply the practice of mindfulness to motherhood. It means we cultivate presence, awareness, and non-judgment, we nurture and resource ourselves, and we do our best to approach our emotions and stress mindfully, so we can parent with empathy, attentiveness, peacefulness, and ease. The following meditations and mantras will help you in this challenging endeavor.

✦ ✧ ✦ ✧ ✦ ✧ ✦ ✧ ✦ ✧ ✦ ✧ ✦ ✧ ✦ ✧ ✦ ✧ ✦ ✧

I AM DOING THE BEST I CAN.

don't "find" time, make time

As mothers, we often put "time for myself" pretty low on our list of priorities. It becomes something to do "when I find the time." But the problem is we never find the time! If we want time to ourselves—to pause and breathe, to take a hot shower, or to savor a cup of coffee—we need to make the time. Pay attention to how you use your time today. Do you notice that there are periods of "wasted" time that could be used for nourishing self-care? Are there commitments that you can drop from your routine? See if you can make time in your day that's just for you!

meditation interruptus

As a mother, the chances that your quiet meditation session will be interrupted are approximately 100 percent. But when your peaceful silence is broken by a young person needing your attention, the meditation doesn't need to end. You can simply shift your awareness from your breath to your child. Mindfulness is about paying attention to whatever is happening right now. During formal practice, breathing is happening, and when your child arrives parenting is happening. You can bring your kind and careful attention to this moment with your child.

keep your sense of humor

You know the phrase, "Some day you'll look back on all this and laugh"? Given what we know about our ability to sustain attention and remember things, we probably won't get around to laughing at it "some day," so why not today? Can you be so present with what's happening that you see not only the difficult, but the hilarious? Yes, it's annoying when you need to leave the house and your five-year-old is running around in his underwear humming the "Star Wars" theme while pretending to wield a light saber, but that's also really funny. So go ahead and laugh.

"I am perfectly imperfect"

There's so much pressure to be a SuperMama, but no mother is perfect. Being mindful doesn't mean we will do everything right, but it will certainly help us stay connected to our intentions. We will bring our loving attention and presence to the important work of mothering. We will notice when we are not acting in a way that aligns with our deepest values, and then we'll hold ourselves with compassion as we begin again. We will notice, too, the moments that feel amazing and delightful, the times when we do feel like a SuperMama, and appreciate our gifts and actions that made those moments possible. Repeat the mantra "I Am Perfectly Imperfect," and remember that this is exactly what your children need you to be.

I DESERVE CARE AND EMPATHY.

"I am at peace in the storm"

Mindful motherhood is about being in the center, about finding the space of calm weather in the eye of the storm. I don't mean you need to find some woo-woo "heart center." I mean you should literally find your center. While the tantrums and mealtimes and arguments and snuggles and messes and kisses swirl around us, we find stability in the center as we embrace the totality of motherhood. You can find this by practicing the introductory exercises in Chapter 1, and through engaging in self-care practices that nourish your soul and allow you to feel stabilized in the midst of chaos and change. Repeat the mantra:

"I Am at Peace in the Storm."

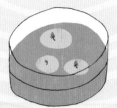

"It's okay"

It's okay to have a day when …

The beds don't get made, but art projects do

•

Soccer practice gets skipped, but long naps don't

•

Popcorn is served for dinner, and ice cream for dessert

•

The to-do list remains long, because our time with
our children is short.

On these days, remember to tell yourself, "It's okay."

phone awareness

Most of us spend too much time on our phones; they are designed to capture our attention, and leave us craving more stimulation. You can bring your mindful awareness to your phone habits by putting a special picture on your lock screen that reminds you to ask yourself, "What am I looking for? What do I need?" when you pick up your phone. If you're looking for directions to a playdate, then your phone is the perfect place to go. If you're looking for connection, or if you're bored or lonely, then maybe the phone isn't really what you need right now. You don't need to ditch your phone all together, but you can be more mindful of what you're using it for. When you put down your phone, notice how you feel. Did you just laugh at a goofy cat video and now you feel relaxed and happy? Great! Did you just check Instagram and now you feel completely miserable and totally inferior after seeing the perfect looking meals and art projects and home repairs all the other mothers are doing? Hmmm … This isn't about judging yourself for being on your phone, but simply taking in the information your body is giving you about how the way you spend your time impacts how you feel.

WHAT DO I NEED?

playing vs winning

Research shows that athletes perform better when they focus on playing to play, instead of playing to win. Instead of trying to get a #motherhoodwin, see if you can just focus on the act of being a mother. Parent in this moment, responding to the needs of this moment, without trying to win the moment. That doesn't mean you can't have intentions for how you will be and how your children will be, but if you focus too intently on winning and arriving at a set destination, you'll miss the journey of getting there, and perhaps a few fun side trips along the way.

empathy does not mean agreement

You can empathize with your child without agreeing
with her or letting her emotions run the show. You
can let your child know you understand that it's hard
to get ready for bed when she's been having fun
playing, but still ensure that she gets to bed on time.
Don't hold back on empathy because you think it
means indulging her whims or agreeing that you are
being "mean." Empathy is an important way of
validating her experience.

change is the only constant

With mindfulness, we embrace change, because it is one of the few things that we know for certain will happen. Just when you get into a groove, or when you think you've figured everything out, things will change again. It's a completely natural and necessary process as you and your children grow and move through the world together. See if you can welcome change as your partner in this unpredictable adventure.

HOW CAN I TAKE CARE OF MYSELF RIGHT NOW?

you don't have to engage your child all the time

Just like you, your child needs quiet time and down time. Even an infant needs wakeful time without stimulation or engagement so that he can curiously and quietly observe his world. Putting pressure on yourself to always entertain and engage your child will exhaust both of you. Ensuring that everyone has down time and some brief alone time during the day will make your playtime that much richer and more enjoyable.

motherhood stories

We all have stories in our mind about what motherhood should be like and how mothers should act, and those stories influence how we feel about ourselves. It's helpful to spend some time considering the things you tell yourself or believe about motherhood, such as "Motherhood should come naturally," or "Good mothers never yell at their children." Sometimes these stories operate under the surface, and cause us a lot of pain when we don't live up to our unstated expectations. The truth is, motherhood will be what it is for you, and the more aware you are of your stories, the less you will add to your own suffering by thinking you are somehow "doing it wrong."

✦ ✦ ✦ ✦ ✦ ✦ ✦ ✦ ✦ ✦ ✦ ✦ ✦ ✦ ✦ ✦ ✦ ✦

when me-time is over

It can be hard to shift back into mothering mode after you've been in "me-time" mode. Mothers tell me that they don't want the bliss of self-care and rest to come to an end, and find themselves dreading the end of their alone time. This is the basis of much of our suffering, when we crave pleasant experiences and then try to hold on to them. See if you can practice being so fully present with "me-time" that there's no grasping—there's just peaceful time to yourself.

a mindful shower

Going to the spa is out of the question most days,
but can you be completely present when you shower
or take a bath? Enjoy the sensation of warm water on
your skin, savor the scent of a favorite body wash,
pay attention to the soothing sounds of running
water. Instead of letting your mind wander to your
to-do list, or running through your day in
your head, just let your shower be a time to wash,
and to care for yourself.

leave work at work

It's hard to arrive home and be fully with your family if your head is still at work. Perhaps it might help to do a "mind dump" before you leave work, writing down all that you need to focus on tomorrow and the things that you don't want to forget. Take a few deep breaths as you think about leaving the work part of your day behind, and transitioning home. Then when you get home, you can be completely present with your children.

knowing your triggers

There are lots of things that can upset us during the day, and it's helpful to know exactly what those things are, because we're often wrong about them. For the next week, keep a "Trigger Tracker" where you write down the specific incidents or behaviors that cause you to "lose it." You might start to notice a pattern: it's always at a particular time of day, or it's because of a particular request, or something else. You may realize that the actual trigger is not what you thought it was (for example, sometimes in my work with mothers, they discover that, with all apologies to the guys out there, it's actually their husbands triggering them, and not their kids!) Take some time to investigate your triggers and see what you notice.

time of day	trigger/ event	reaction	what I noticed

two-minute self-care

Self-care doesn't have to be extensive or expensive. There are lots of things you can do in just two minutes (or less) that can nourish you and give you some refueling during your day. If you have just two minutes, you can:

Drink a full glass of water

•

Step outside and take some deep breaths

•

Close your eyes and breathe

•

Call or text a friend

•

Listen to your favorite song

•

Do a few gentle yoga stretches or poses.

CHAPTER 4

SUSTAIN

MINDFULNESS THROUGHOUT THE DAY

Mindfulness is both a formal practice, and something we cultivate throughout the day. Mindfulness teacher Jon Kabat-Zinn likes to ask, "When does the meditation end?" Just because we've gotten up from our cushion doesn't mean we fall back into our regular mode of distraction and over-reaction. Use the practices in this chapter to sustain your mindfulness practice over the course of your day.

drop in

At any moment of your day, you can "drop in": drop in to your body and notice what you are feeling. Notice your feet on the floor. Notice where you are and what you are doing. Just drop in to presence.

nap-time meditation

If your children still take naps, use nap time as a moment of quiet reflection for yourself. Close your eyes and take a few (or many!) deep breaths. What has gone well so far today? What can you honor yourself for doing? Take a moment to soak in the good that has already happened. Consider what has been difficult today, and what you can do in the remaining hours to take care of yourself as you care for your child.

the best time of day for meditation

The best time of day for meditation is the time of day when you will meditate—i.e. it is different for everyone. I prefer early morning, because the house is quiet, and I like knowing that the first thing I do in the day is just for me. But you need to find the time that will work for you. When are you most alert and least likely to get interrupted? It's helpful to pick a time that's relatively consistent, as this will help you keep your habit going. If morning doesn't work for you, see if you can practice during your lunchtime, during nap time, or before bed.

WHAT IS MY INTENTION RIGHT NOW?

come home to yourself

No matter how far you travel and all the places you go throughout your day, you can come home to yourself at any time. Take a deep breath and bring your mind and body into the same place. Gently touching or lightly tapping your arms, legs, face, or shoulders can help you awaken the body, orient you to your environment, and create a moment of embodied presence.

✦ ✦ ✦ ✦ ✦ ✦ ✦ ✦ ✦ ✦ ✦ ✦ ✦ ✦ ✦ ✦ ✦ ✦

mindful cleaning

The repetitive movements of cleaning your home can be a soothing meditation if you choose to make them so. As you tidy up today, bring your awareness to the movements of your body. Notice the sights and smells and sounds around you. Take a moment to express gratitude for the spaces and objects you are cleaning. Your daily chores can be drudgery—or you can make them a special practice in caring for your home and protecting those who live in it with you. The choice is yours.

one mindful activity

Choose one activity today that you will do with complete presence and attention. Try to pick something that you often do mind-less-ly, such as loading the dishwasher, preparing a bottle, folding the laundry, or walking to your desk at work. Pay attention to the movements of your body, your internal sensations, and the sounds and sights and smells around you. Notice what it's like to be completely present in very ordinary moments.

WHAT IS HAPPENING IN MY BODY RIGHT NOW?

I WILL MOVE THROUGH MY DAY WITH AWARENESS AND ATTENTION.

slow down

See if there is a part of your day that you can deliberately slow down. It might be washing the dishes or making lunches more slowly, or it could be walking at a more regular pace rather than speed walking to the store or to your place of work. You don't need to go obnoxiously slow—try to go about 70 percent of your regular speed. What does it feel like to slow down? If you're usually really fast (like most of us are), you might discover that it's actually quite normal and acceptable, and in fact a bit pleasanter, to move slightly less forcefully through the world. (If you find you prefer hurried movement, that's okay too. The point is to be mindful of what you do, no matter what your pace).

mindful exercise

Make your workouts mindful. Ditch the headphones and turn off the TV, and focus your attention on your amazing body and your powerful muscles and all the incredible things you can do with them.

stir the rice mindfully

Mindfulness teacher Sharon Salzberg tells the story of a wise mother who was super-busy with many children, and yet was completely mindful and present. When asked how she had time to meditate with all those kids around, the woman explained that she simply stirred the rice mindfully. You may not have time for meditation today, or even tomorrow. But can you stir the rice mindfully? Can you make the lunches mindfully? Can you give your child a bath mindfully?

it's okay to love the times when you're away

Sometimes mothers feel they must "confess" to me that they love it when they have the house to themselves, or when they go to work and have adult conversations for several hours, or even when they go to the grocery store by themselves. But this needn't be a confession—it's not a sin to cherish the time that's just for you. Someday your children will no longer need your daily care, and now is the time when it's important to nurture your own interests and your relationship with yourself so you are still fully here when that day arrives.

I CAN MAKE ANY MOMENT
A MINDFUL MOMENT

what's my motivation?

Try to get into the habit of checking in with your motivation for the actions you take. Every move has an intention behind it, whether we are aware of it or not. Is your question "What should we do today?" an invitation for everyone to share their input, or an attempt to steer them to your agenda? Today, practice noticing the brief moments before you act. Investigate what has prompted your desire to act, what thoughts you're having about what the outcome will be, and whether the action you are about to take is one that is necessary and helpful in that moment. You might be surprised by how many times you act without thinking, or how some behaviors may be prompted by unskillful motivations. This isn't about judging or criticizing yourself. Think of it as gathering data to help you cultivate the insight that will help you act the way you want to in the world.

fab five

The moment when everyone arrives home after school or after work can be a challenging time, so try implementing the "Fab Five." For the first five minutes when everyone is reunited, the focus is simply on connecting: hugs and kisses, how are yous and I missed yous. There's no opening the mail, rushing to make dinner, nagging about homework, checking email, or tidying the morning mess. There will be time for all that later; for the minutes of the "Fab Five," it's just about reconnecting with the ones you love.

✦ ✦ ✦ ✦ ✦ ✦ ✦ ✦ ✦ ✦ ✦ ✦ ✦ ✦ ✦ ✦ ✦ ✦

be still

For one whole minute today, just be still.
No movement, no noise. Just be still.

change it up

We are creatures of habit—every day we might eat the same breakfast, drive the same way to work, park in the same spot, and walk the same route with the dogs. It's not that habits are bad (indeed, having some things on auto-pilot frees up space in our head for more complicated activities). But habits can prevent us from engaging with our life with awareness. Today, see if you can change up a habit—brush your teeth with the opposite hand, sit in a different spot in your meeting, walk a different way to the park. See what you notice when you're not on auto-pilot.

are you pounding the pavement?

I mean that question literally—when you walk around during the day, do you pound the pavement, slamming your feet into the ground instead of lightly stepping on the earth? You can cause yourself all sorts of aches and pains when you walk with heavy legs and feet, which sends a jarring impact through your spine. Can you try walking softly today, imagining that your feet and legs are weightless as you bring them to the ground?

✦ ✦ ✦ ✦ ✦ ✦ ✦ ✦ ✦ ✦ ✦ ✦ ✦ ✦ ✦ ✦

chest openers

Chest openers are a great exercise for all of us, but especially nursing mothers. We spend much of our day hunched over a baby, a toddler, or a computer, and it takes a toll on our back. Often, we aren't even aware of the tension in our body until we collapse into bed, achy and exhausted. Simple exercises throughout the day can help us release these tensions. Try standing up and stretching your arms behind you, clasping your hands together if you can. Lift your head and chest and pull your shoulders back. Do these several times a day when you need a quick stretch.

standing meditation

Meditation is said to happen in four main postures: sitting, lying, walking, and standing. As so much of parenting is done literally on your feet, it can help to try a standing meditation. To do this (a great time is when you're waiting in line at the store), notice your feet grounding into the floor. Put down baskets or bags and slowly shift your weight from side to side, feeling the earth support you. Gently bend your knees, and tuck your pelvis in to reduce strain on your back. Roll your shoulders up and back and allow your arms to hang effortlessly at your side.

who's driving?

Throughout your day, ask yourself, "Who's driving?" Are you present and in control, making decisions with awareness and intention? Or has your auto-pilot taken over, leading you to make careless mistakes or be driven by habitual reactions? When you notice your inner chauffeur has taken the wheel on a route she's not really equipped for, see if you can get yourself back in the driver's seat.

CHAPTER 5

SUPPORT

MINDFULNESS FOR DIFFICULT MOMENTS

Raising little people is hard work, which means as a mother there will be no shortage of opportunities to practice working with difficulty. The meditations in the previous chapters are the practice for the stuff we need to deal with here: how to keep our cool when our children get fired up and start pushing buttons we didn't even know we had. When these difficult moments arise, you have a choice: how are you going to be with them? Are you going to fight the difficulty? Are you going to kick and scream at it? Are you going to wish it away? Or are you going to allow it, get curious about it, and then see what happens in the next moment? The meditations and practices in this chapter will help you in doing the latter, so you can meet the hard parts of motherhood with greater ease.

what do I control?

Sometimes you can take refuge in Reinhold Neibuhr's Serenity Prayer, which counsels us to change the things we can change, and to accept the things we cannot. If you've hit a tough moment, ask yourself, "What do I control?" There's a lot you do not control the weather, traffic, viruses, homework, or your child's behavior, to name just a few. But in every moment, there is at least something you can control—perhaps it's your response, your attitude, or simply your breath. Take a deep breath, and allow the things you don't control to be as they are. Take another deep breath, and engage in wise action toward the things you do control.

MY PRESENCE IS ENOUGH.

don't bake the cake

Be mindful of what you can realistically achieve in the time you have available. You may decide to go all out and bake a Pinterest worthy birthday cake for your child's party, complete with matching homemade decorations. But if in doing so you stress yourself out, and don't have enough time to wrap the presents, prepare the goodie bags, and clean the house, you'll just make yourself miserable. Be mindful of what you have the time and energy to do. Go ahead and buy a cake if you don't have time to bake the cake!

I CAN HANDLE THIS.

begin again

Every moment of every day is a chance to make a fresh
start. Each moment is an opportunity to pause, to apologize,
to help, to listen. Each moment is an invitation to revisit your
intentions and begin again.

don't cry over spilled milk

When milk has spilled onto the kitchen floor, what is needed of you? You need to clean up the milk. You can't go back in time and unspill the milk. You can't yell at the milk (well, you can … but let me know how that goes). What you can do is clean up the milk. You can clean up the milk with anger and resentment, or you can clean up the milk with presence and without judgment. You can clean up the milk and let your mind go wild with irritating thoughts of how many more times you'll be cleaning up spilled milk and other fluids today. Or you can clean up the milk with thoughts about cleaning up this milk from this floor right now. The choice is yours.

it's okay not to love every minute of it

Well-meaning acquaintances often ask mothers, "Don't you just love every minute of it?" And while there is much to love about motherhood, it's hard to love every minute of it. Some parts—ugly tantrums, bedtime battles, potty training—are downright miserable, and thinking that you're supposed to be loving it only makes it worse. Whatever response you are having to the present moment is completely acceptable, because it's the response you are having! Just because things are difficult and uncomfortable right now doesn't mean that you don't love being a mother, or that you don't love your children—it just means it's hard right now.

overwhelm

Mothers constantly tell me they are overwhelmed. Mindfulness teacher Shinzen Young says that overwhelm is a "loss of sensory discrimination"—we become so flooded with sensations that we cannot separate or distinguish them. With mindful awareness, we cultivate the ability to break down our emotions into distinct sensory events. When you feel overwhelmed today, see if you can stop and identify the component parts of your experience.

What bodily sensations are present?

•

What's happening in your mind?

Seeing the moment as a composition of various sensations, thoughts, memories, and judgments makes it much more manageable than a vague, but powerful, feeling of "overwhelm."

WHAT CAN I LEARN FROM THIS?

✦ ✦ ✦ ✦ ✦ ✦ ✦ ✦ ✦ ✦ ✦ ✦ ✦ ✦ ✦ ✦ ✦ ✦

time-outs aren't just for kids anymore!

When things get really tense and heated, you can call a time-out for everyone—you, the kids, even the dog. A time-out isn't a punishment. It's a time to stop, step back from the intensity of a difficult moment, and breathe. When you sense everyone just needs a break today, call "Time out!" and allow everyone, including you, a chance to close their eyes and reset. (See the next chapter for soothing practices to do with your child in these time-outs.)

✦ ✦ ✦ ✦ ✦ ✦ ✦ ✦ ✦ ✦ ✦ ✦ ✦ ✦ ✦ ✦ ✦ ✦

all the other mothers

If you are struggling with something today, you can guarantee that another mother is struggling with it, too. Throughout history, women have faced the daunting task of nurturing little people and helping them become competent big people. You may not see the other mothers today, but you share a bond with them that stretches for millennia. What you are struggling with, they have struggled with. Your struggles are part of the human condition, which means they are normal, universal, and completely deal-with-able.

hold space

When your child is having a difficult time, he needs you to hold space for him. Holding space for another person means we allow that person to have the experience he is having, without judgment, and without running away. We let him know that we can handle this difficulty together. When your child gets frustrated that he can't tie his shoes fast enough, you might be tempted to leave him "until he can do it without whining." What if, instead, you held space for him by being a calm presence next to him, offering encouragement with your words or simply your relaxed nervous system? When he sees you can tolerate frustration, he can begin to learn to tolerate it, too. In the same way, when your child is fired up, he doesn't really need your words, he needs your stable, attuned presence. See if you can resist the urge to lecture, to explain that this isn't a big deal, or describe how he could be handling things better. Just stay with him, offering a hug or a soft touch if he will allow it. If he's too fired up to let you get close, stay near to him and breathe slowly (perhaps exaggerating your deep breaths as a demonstration). Your stable, non-judging presence is usually the most helpful thing you can offer.

learning from a difficult moment

After a difficult experience with your child, you may just want to forget about it and move on. But you can bring your mindful, nonjudgmental awareness to the encounter, reviewing what happened just before things went downhill. How were you feeling physically: Hungry, tired, or rested? How were you feeling emotionally? What were you thinking about? Were you present? Can you replay the moment and identify the specific behavior or incident that "triggered" you? How did it make you feel? What was happening in your body? What thoughts arose? Can you identify the moment when you could have chosen to respond in a different way? This isn't about blaming yourself—it's about becoming familiar with the things that upset you, and how you react. It's about locating those small, choice-full moments—even retroactively—so you can handle a similar situation differently the next time.

dealing with stress

"top down" practices

MEANING:
Is there something I can learn from this?

REFRAME:
Is there another way to look at this?

MEMORY:
How have I dealt with this in the past?

"bottom up" practices

BREATHE:
Breathe from the belly.
Lengthen the exhale.

EMBODY:
Sit up.
Move.
Exercise.

children will be childish

Sometimes I just need to remind myself that. It's simply in the
nature of a one-year-old to make a mess and play loudly. It's in the
nature of a four-year-old to move slowly, and sometimes clumsily.
It's in the nature of a seven-year-old to find bodily functions
humorous. Instead of getting frustrated that this little person does
not yet act like an adult, see if you can find something to celebrate
about who he is now, and treasure his childness. For tomorrow he'll
already be a little bit older.

I DON' T LIKE THIS. BUT I

CAN BE WITH IT.

don't resist

When your day doesn't go according to plan, you have two choices: resist, or go with it. So often, our first instinct is to resist ("I don't want it to be this way," "I wanted this to happen instead.") But resisting what is happening—resisting the present moment—is exhausting. When your day gets derailed, take a deep breath, and instead of fighting the present moment, see if you can soften into it.

this child, this moment

When your child is having one of those moments, your only task is to parent this child in this moment. While your thoughts might drift to all the other times she's behaved in this way, or all the times she may do so in the future, all you can respond to right now is this behavior from this child in this moment. It doesn't mean you can't address the underlying issues later, but right now, just focus on this moment.

misbehavior is an invitation

With mindful awareness and patience, we can see our child's misbehavior as an invitation. It's an invitation to consider what our child needs in this moment. Most kids know how they're supposed to behave, and they generally want to behave in that way, so when that behavior doesn't happen, it's an invitation for us to be curious. What need of hers is not being met? Accept the invitation, and find out.

your life is real

You'll drive yourself crazy comparing yourself to the mothers in magazines or in your Pinterest feed. There's no one perfect way to mother, and your child will develop according to his own timeline, not the one outlined in a parenting article. Advertisements and social media are not intended to be a reflection of reality and shouldn't be taken as such. Resist comparing yourself to anyone else.

you get to choose

In any given moment, you can choose your:

Attitude

•

Words

•

Actions

It's an incredible power. Choose joyfully,
with presence and wisdom.

forgiveness meditation

If you are struggling with your feelings of being hurt
by someone, see if you can practice a silent
forgiveness meditation. Bring to mind the person
you want or need to forgive—it may be your child,
your partner, a friend, or even yourself. Notice any
negative judgments or thoughts that arise. Silently
say to this person, "I forgive you. If you could have
done better, in that moment, you would have."
Forgiving someone doesn't mean you are condoning
what she did or releasing her from the consequences
of her action. It means you are releasing yourself
from resentment and anger. Forgiveness can be a
difficult practice, and it may help to repeat this
exercise a few times.

everyone's hard is hard

It's tempting to try to talk yourself out of feeling upset when there are people who are in much worse situations than you are all over the globe. But you know what? Everyone's hard is hard. If it's hard for you, then it's hard. You needn't feel guilty for acknowledging your own pain and difficulty; in fact, that's how you will strengthen yourself so that you may help others.

it gets better

If there's one thing I know for certain from my own motherhood experience, it's that it gets better. The sleepless nights don't last forever, the battles over naps and potty-training will one day be a distant memory, and eventually this helpless little tot will be able to feed and dress herself … and even drive! As she gets older and you get wiser and you both get to know each other better.

it's okay to be wrong

No one—not even your children—expects you to have all the answers and always to get it right. It's okay not to know the solutions to the homework. It's okay to make mistakes. We all do. It's okay to realize you could have done it better. Remember that we want our children to know it's okay to get things wrong sometimes, and we should extend that same kindness and leniency to ourselves.

some days are just not happy days

Mindfulness is not going to make us happy all the time (nor, really, would we want it to). Some days, honestly, are just miserable the kids are cranky, we're cranky, and nothing turns out as we expected. That's just how some days are. If it's a hard day, just sit with your hard day. It won't last.

tantrum meditation

If we could rank mindfulness practices from beginner to total ninja, staying mindfully calm and present during a loud, screaming tantrum would absolutely qualify you for a black belt. If tantrums trigger you, welcome to the club! The next time your child starts firing on all cylinders, see if you can act as the brakes. First, take a deep breath and ground yourself by feeling your feet, noticing how they anchor you in place. Allow that to be the stable base you stand on, projecting calm and presence as your child rages; this lets your child know that you can handle this moment, even if she cannot. As best you can, see if you can observe the tantrum not as the parent trying to "fix" it, but as an outsider. Be curious about the tantrum: Can you identify the need your child is trying to meet? Can you identify the moment the tantrum "peaks," when your child's energy shifts and she is ready to hear your soothing and comforting voice? As with any training, the Tantrum Meditation takes practice, but over time see if you notice yourself being less reactive and more intentionally aware during these difficult parenting moments. Notice the impact your presence has on your child.

IF IT'S HARD FOR ME, IT'S HARD FOR OTHER MOTHERS, TOO.

reframing

Psychologists tell us that many of our problems can become less overwhelming if we can reframe them, for there are many vantage points from which a situation can be viewed. When you're stuck in resentment or worry or frustration, ask yourself if you can put this scenario in a different frame. Is this child willful and stubborn, or is he passionate and confident? Is this another half hour of drudgery in the kitchen, or an opportunity to nurture your family's physical and emotional health through a home-made meal? The choice is yours.

they are not their tantrums

A tough truth about motherhood is that the times when our children most need our loving attention and support are the times when their behaviors are the least likely to evoke tenderness in us. A child throwing a tantrum needs your presence, and it can be easier to offer it if you remind yourself that "My child is not her tantrum." The tantrum is an outward manifestation of the big emotions her little body is struggling to process. Can you see the sweet child beneath the surface behavior? Can you hold space with her (see page 82) as this storm passes through her?

"I am doing the important work"

Mothers often tell me that one of their biggest frustrations is feeling like they have nothing to show for all the work they do. But mindfulness is about not attaching to outcomes: we do something because it is meaningful or necessary, without holding tightly to an expected result. And that's a lot of what motherhood is! Mothering cannot be measured in profit and loss charts or tallies of widgets made. The important work of mothering is mothering itself: the tending and feeding and singing and hugging and redirecting and bathing and teaching and laughing and boo-boo kissing. You are doing the important work, Mama, so tell yourself that!

don't take it personally

Motherhood is an incredibly personal act, but sometimes we need not to take it so personally. When your child is upset, or misbehaving, or otherwise acting unskillfully, it's usually not about you. Even when she tells you you're the worst mother in the world, it's still not really about you. Her young mind and little body are dealing with big emotions and complicated rules, which can provoke all sorts of unskillful words and behaviors. There will be time later, when she has calmed down, that you can talk about behaviors and consequences, but for now, don't take it personally. Right now, she needs you to be the safe container to help her hold this difficult experience.

all the terrible things

Mark Twain supposedly once quipped, "I've been through a lot of terrible things in my life, some of which actually happened." Can you notice the times when you allow yourself to get completely caught up in the drama and trauma of an event that is not actually happening? When you catch yourself doing this, see if you can remember Twain's mocking words, and remind yourself to focus on what is actually happening.

✦ ✦ ✦ ✦ ✦ ✦ ✦ ✦ ✦ ✦ ✦ ✦ ✦ ✦ ✦ ✦ ✦ ✦

resentment

Resentment may be one of the most difficult experiences for us to work with as mothers, because it can lead to intense feelings of guilt. But it is a completely normal and quite common feeling—our children demand so much of us, and it can be incredibly overwhelming at times. We may long for our easy, kid-free days, or wish that everything would just be quiet, or we might miss the independence we once had. When resentment arises, be compassionate with yourself. Can you sense what need of yours is not being met? Do you know what you could do to meet that need?

charming chatterbox

Little kids like to tell stories, often the same stories, over and over and over again. There may be days when you just want your little chatterbox to get to the point and wrap it up so you can have a few moments of silence. When this happens, notice your irritation and see if you can summon the patience for another round of "the cool world I just built in Minecraft." Your child wants to share his world and his ideas with you. Can you see the charm in your chatterbox? Can you appreciate that one day, he may not be so chatty, and you might miss these moments?

find the yes in the no

If children are masters at uttering one word, it's "no." And that one word can trigger mothers like no other. But when your child says "no" to something, he's also saying "yes" to something else. A "no" to cleaning up toys is perhaps a "yes" to more playtime. You don't have to indulge your child's defiance, but you can be mindful of your child's needs in this moment. Instead of fighting back with a "Yes, you will clean up your toys," you can say, "We'll have more time for playing cars after dinner, but right now we need to clean up for lunch." For today, determine what your child is saying "yes" to when he says "no," and see if it helps to defuse tense moments.

I WILL CHOOSE TO SEE IT
THIS WAY INSTEAD.

I won't always try to fix it

When your child is really upset, what she needs is not your answers, your fixing, your moralizing, or your stories. What she needs is your permission to have her experience. She wants and needs you to hear her words with presence and empathy. She needs the safe space to feel what she's feeling. In these moments, what she needs from you is complete, silent, whole-body listening, without judgment, questioning, or advice. She simply needs you to meet her where she's at with empathy. (See also Allow Silence on page 111.) So however hard it is to hold back, tell yourself you're not going to try to fix it today.

meaning

Psychiatrist and Holocaust survivor Victor Frankl has said that "suffering ceases to be suffering at the moment it finds a meaning." When things are hard, can you find the meaning? Is there a lesson to be learned, a new direction to be explored? The meaning of a particularly difficult time in your life may not be readily apparent, but you can probably think of harrowing times in your past that helped shape you into who you are today. Can you trust that if the meaning is not discernible right now, it will be some day?

insight meditation

Mindfulness meditation is sometimes called "insight meditation," which is a perfect description of the practice: we pay attention in order to cultivate insight and wisdom. Through carefully attending to your experience, you may discover that you hit the same problems every week. Think of this as an invitation to consider possible solutions. Can homework be done at a different time of the afternoon? If your child is resisting going to dance lessons, is it time to call it quits and find an activity that better meets her interests? When you start to see all your experiences as data, you can figure out what's working, what's NOT working, and find new solutions.

loving kindness for your child

This meditation can be really helpful to do on a day—or during a phase—that is difficult for you and your child. Take a deep breath, and bring an image of your child to your mind. Really picture him—what's he doing, what's he wearing, what's the expression on his face? Place your hands on your heart, and silently repeat the following phrases to yourself, imagining that you are sending these wishes straight to your child:

May you be happy

•

May you be safe

•

May you be healthy

•

May you be loved

Take another deep breath and notice what it feels like to send these kind thoughts to your child.

❖❖❖❖❖❖❖❖❖❖❖❖❖❖❖❖❖❖❖

CHAPTER 6

TOGETHER TIME

MINDFULNESS WITH YOUR KIDS

Adults who discover the practice of mindfulness quickly recognize that it would have been a powerful tool to have as a kid. The most effective way you can teach your children mindfulness is by example. Through your calm presence, deliberate pauses, carefully chosen words, and genuine empathy, you will model what it means to pay attention with love and curiosity. Right now, you may just want to focus on your own practice, and that's totally okay. It's important that you feel comfortable with mindfulness before you try to teach it to your kids. When you're ready, you'll find that teaching mindfulness strategies to your children will help them be more focused and attentive.

❖❖❖❖❖❖❖❖❖❖❖❖❖❖❖❖❖❖

just trying to get my attention

Sometimes we say that when a child is misbehaving, they are "just trying to get my attention." And we're right—they want our attention. They need our attention. As Zen teacher John Tarrant says, "attention is the most basic form of love." We show our children how much they mean to us and how special they are by giving them our undivided and loving attention. This doesn't mean they need 100 percent of our attention 100 percent of the time—that's neither healthy nor possible. But their need for our attention is primal and powerful. Be mindful of giving your child your loving attention throughout your day.

just hug

When we give and receive hugs, our body releases oxytocin, a hormone that promotes bonding and trust. This makes us feel good and relaxed. So give your child a hug, or even give yourself a hug! (Your neurons don't know it's you, so you'll still get a juicy dose of happy hormones if the hug comes from you.)

the 300th round of candyland

You've probably played Candyland (or trucks or Barbies) at least 300 times. It's easy to grow weary of it. But you've never played on this day, with this child, who is just a little bit different from the way she was yesterday. So play. Notice your child's face and words and actions. Be present. You'll never play this 300th round of Candyland again.

✦ ✦ ✦ ✦ ✦ ✦ ✦ ✦ ✦ ✦ ✦ ✦ ✦ ✦ ✦ ✦ ✦

it's hard to follow rules all day

From the moment our children enter preschool, they are following rules and "holding it together" for a long time every day. When they get home, it's natural for tears, frustration, attitude, and misbehavior to "leak" out, after being contained all day. In some ways, at-home meltdowns are a good thing—they are a sign of our children's absolute faith in us, their confidence that we will stick by them no matter how messy things get. When things get rough after school, repeat the mantra "It's Hard to Follow the Rules All Day," and cultivate some empathy for your child.

I CAN CHOOSE MY ACTIONS AND MY BELIEFS.

free time

My children and I like to have "free time"—we set aside several hours on a weekend when I have to say "Yes" to everything they ask to do that is:

1) screen-free and

2) actually free.

We play board games, bake cookies, make crafts, read books, take naps, or walk the dogs. We can be completely present with each other as we enjoy some simple pleasures.

be in the moment with your child

I remember one night when my son was aged four, and I was feeling particularly impatient about getting him to bed. He was moving too slowly for my agenda, and I noticed my irritation and the stories in my head: "He's always dawdling. I just want some time to myself and he's purposely stalling." Remembering to be mindful, I took a deep breath and really looked at him. I watched him play with how he could stretch his legs as he put on his pajamas, listened to him sing a gentle "loo-la-da-di-dahh …" as he readied himself for bed, and observed him curiously studying a small imperfection in the carpet by his tiny feet. He was totally and completely in the moment, mindful of his body and his surroundings. With mindfulness, I was able to join him in this precious moment.

happy days

Make a list with your kids of the things you can do as a family that make you happy—going to the movies, coloring together, snuggling on the couch, going for a walk, playing a game. On a day when not much is scheduled, declare a "Happy Day!" Each person in the family gets to pick one item on the list for everyone to do together. If you'd like, you can talk about why these things feel good.

allow silence

When you are with your child, and the conversation stalls, see if you can allow the silence. Your natural tendency may be to fill the moment with more talk and activity, but often the quiet serves as an invitation for your child to open up. This can be especially powerful when you are helping your child through a difficult situation. Instead of immediately trying to "fix" things, if you sit in silence and see what emerges, you might find that your child opens up to you and that you learn a lot more from her.

be mindful for your kids

Children have a hard time identifying their emotions. You can bring your mindful awareness to their experience by naming what is present. For example, when your child is getting upset, you could say, "It looks like you're feeling frustrated because Amy said she didn't want to share her doll with you. I bet you wish you two could play with it together." When you do this, you not only show empathy, but you help your child understand her emotions, needs, and desires in a way that she might not be able to verbalize yet.

reading mindfully

Story time can be a great opportunity to have conversations about difficult emotions and experiences because your children can talk about the problems of fictional characters, instead of diving into their own messy and complicated feelings. They might even get some clarity or better understanding of their own experience by reflecting on the stories you read. You can ask your child questions such as, "Why do you think the boy is feeling sad?" "What do you think made the bunny so angry?" These questions can open up a powerful dialog with your kids about emotions, behavior, and motivations.

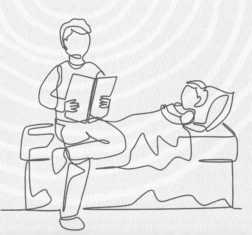

family gratitude journal

Get a special notebook to keep in the kitchen or somewhere everyone will be able to find it, and make it a Family Gratitude Journal. Anyone can write in it about what they are thankful for. It's especially sweet to encourage your children to write down the nice things that other family members do for them, or what they appreciate about their family. Set aside some special nights during the year to read through the family journal.

◇ ◇ ◇ ◇ ◇ ◇ ◇ ◇ ◇ ◇ ◇ ◇ ◇ ◇ ◇

no-phone zone

If you're in the habit of carrying your phone around the house with you, see if you can make bedtime a "no-phone zone." It's hard to be mindful and in the moment during bathtime, story time, and cuddle time with a buzzing phone constantly interrupting you. While you're at it, see if you can make your bedtime routine a no-phone zone—you'll rest a lot better at night if you're not stimulating your mind with brightly-lit news and emails right before bed.

silence isn't silent

Sit with your child and set a timer for 30 seconds. Tell your child that you are both going to be as quiet as possible for 30 seconds (you can try to make it a challenge if you think that will be hard for your little one!), and you are going to listen to all the sounds around you while you are silent. After the timer goes off, see if you can identify five things you heard. This gives your child practice in paying attention.

I CAN TAKE MY FAMILY'S
LOVE WITH ME
THROUGHOUT MY DAY.

mindful
story time

You might be dreadfully exhausted when evening story time rolls around. This sometimes leads to inattention and frustration during what could be a sweet and tender closing moment for your day with your child. Tonight, bring your awareness to story time. Notice when your attention wanders, when your mouth is saying the words but your mind is miles away, thinking of to-do lists and upcoming meetings. See if you can bring your attention back to your body, back to sitting on this bed, back to the story, and back to your child.

bedtime body scan

This is a really helpful practice for a child
who is having trouble falling asleep at
night. Invite him to lie down on his
back in bed, and imagine that there
is a soothing, softly glowing light
down by his feet. Ask him to
imagine that this light provides a
safe and soothing warmth as it
moves gently over his body. While the
light is at his feet, have him sense his
feet and allow them to relax, gently letting
the feet spread apart as this light protects them.
Then ask him to envision the light slowly traveling up his legs,
to his knees, thighs, and hips. As the light comes over his
belly, it helps him soften his upper body and breathe slowly
and deeply. Continue bringing the light all the way up his
torso, arms, neck, and face. This gentle light can envelop his
body as he sleeps safely through the night.

the train of thought

In the delightful Pixar movie *Inside Out*, the human mind is shown as literally having a "train of thought." This is a great visual representation of how thoughts run through the mind. If you have a toy train (preferably one with multiple cars), use that to demonstrate to your child how thoughts can move fast or slow, can be big or little, and can be colorful or dark. Tell your child to imagine that when she notices her thoughts, she is just watching a train go by with lots of ideas and words packed into the cars. She doesn't have to ride the train and get carried away by her thoughts; she can just watch it go by.

◇ ◇ ◇ ◇ ◇ ◇ ◇ ◇ ◇ ◇ ◇ ◇ ◇ ◇ ◇ ◇ ◇ ◇ ◇ ◇

dynamite!

This practice comes entirely from my son. When he was aged six, he put together a bundle of dynamite sticks made out of construction paper. If he got really upset about something, he would grab his fake dynamite sticks as he sensed his anger rising, and then he'd breathe as he gently relaxed his hold on the dynamite. He would allow the bundle to fall to the ground as he released his anger. Ask your child what his anger looks or feels like: Dynamite? A fist? A lion? A tornado? Have him craft a representation of his anger that he can use to visualize the process of holding his emotional experience and then loosening his grip on it.

cooking together

One way to beat the dinner-time craziness is to invite your children to help you. Depending on their ages, your children can set the table, stir ingredients, measure ingredients, or read the recipe to you. Cooking is an activity that engages all the senses—sight, smell, touch, hearing, and taste; you can talk with your children about all the sensory elements involved in making dinner.

dance party

Put on some fun tunes and bust a move with your kids. Turn up the volume, sing along to the music, and dance your heart out. It's great exercise, and dance is a powerful way to bring your mind and body into the same place as you move in sync with the sounds around you.

simon says

This traditional childhood game actually teaches children several important attentional skills: the ability to understand rules and adjust their behavior when the rules change; the ability to focus their concentration on a single task; the ability to control impulses; and the ability to hold information in working memory. Who knew?! You can make Simon Says easy or complicated based on the ages of your kids, but the premise is simple: the person playing Simon gives instructions ("touch your head," "turn in a circle," etc.), but the players do the action only if he says "Simon says touch your head." When kids get it wrong, use the mistake as an opportunity to talk about how hard it is not to act when we're given an instruction, and how we need to inhibit that impulse. You can also change the rules from time to time. ("Now we do the action if he doesn't say Simon says!") Have fun with it!

my amazing emotions

It's hard to watch our children struggle with big emotions, but there are ways we can help them process and begin to understand their own feelings. Depending on your child's age, when she is grappling with a difficult emotion, you can ask her questions such as: What color is this feeling? What does it look like? Does it have a name? What kind of animal would it be? What is the animal doing? You can invite younger kids to act out the animal/emotion, which can provide some relief from the overwhelming physical sensations of the feeling, and also help them get a better sense of what exactly they're experiencing. With older kids, you can ask questions such as: What kind of action does it feel like your body wants to take? If you could give a label to this emotion, what would it be?

music jam

Gather your musical instruments, or simply find items around the house that can make some noise (you can drum with pencils, tap glasses with spoons, pluck rubber bands, or shake some spice jars). Have one person start a rhythm, and then ask everyone else to join in when they're ready. This is a fun game, and also a powerful way to attune to others by getting in sync with their sounds and movements. And you can create some amazing tunes in your free-flowing jam.

"it's just mini-golf "

The first time I took my children mini-golfing was a disaster. Of course I imagined it would be idyllic fun—the kids and I would navigate windmills and toadstools and all sorts of brightly colored obstacles on a sunny day, while learning a little bit of hand-eye coordination along the way. But I managed to turn it into a stressful golf lesson, focusing all too intently on my children's technique and swing and grip … and I've never actually been real golfing! Somehow I couldn't just let us play; I had to bring precision and rules and structure to something that is intended to be completely wacky and unpredictable. Now when I'm trying to turn play into work, and adding unnecessary complication to something simple, I repeat the mantra "It's Just Mini-Golf."

sitting with your child

Depending on the age of your child, you can invite her to sit in meditation with you. You may want to start with just two or three minutes if she's never tried meditation before. A sweet way to do this is to have her sit on your lap, with her back against your chest. Tell her that you are going to sit for a few minutes and breathe together, just noticing how our bodies feel when we breathe.

I CAN BE KIND TO
SOMEONE ELSE TODAY.

I spy

This is a fun activity to do with your child. Put on your top-secret spy senses, and see if you can spy …

5 things you can see right now

•

4 sounds you can hear right now

•

3 smells you can detect right now

•

2 sensations you can feel right now

•

1 thing you can taste right now.

mindful dinnertime

Try having a mindful family dinner. Each person can share what they are thankful for, and then you can eat your meal together mindfully. Talk about where the food came from and all the work that went into getting this meal to your table. See if everyone can eat in silence for the first three minutes, and then talk about what you notice when you eat slowly and mindfully.

rainbow meditation

Hone your mindful observation skills—and your child's—by seeing how quickly you can find every color in the rainbow in the space around you right now. This is an excellent game to engage your children while you're driving in the car.

emotion charade

To help kids understand how our emotions live in our bodies and express themselves through our faces and actions, you can play Emotion Charades. It's quite simple: someone acts out an emotion in complete silence, using posture, facial expressions, and movements. And everyone tries to guess what the emotion is. You can also engage your children about where in their bodies they feel that emotion.

techy mindfulness with your teen

Teens probably don't want to play mindfulness games, but that doesn't mean they couldn't use some mindfulness. You can introduce your teen to mindfulness through apps designed especially for him, such as "Stop, Breathe, and Think," or "Smiling Mind."

CHAPTER 7

SAVOR
MINDFUL APPRECIATION

Our brains have what psychologists call a "negativity bias," which means we pay more attention to negative events than positive ones. This serves an evolutionary purpose, because it means we're attentive to danger, but sadly it also means we miss out on a lot of the small, ordinary joys. In this chapter, you'll learn practices that will help you pay more attention to the good (which is really good for you), and how to savor the fleeting moments of beauty that make motherhood so incredibly powerful.

hear her sing

The next time you hear your child singing, pause and really listen, as if you're taking a mental recording. Notice the words and tones and vibrations her body is producing. Take a moment to appreciate the innocent and vulnerable high-pitched sound of a child's voice. Hear how she pronounces the words, and see if she makes up her own lyrics. Let the melody she sings linger in your awareness.

smile

Research shows that smiling makes you feel happier. Take a deep breath in, and on the exhale, bring your lips into a slight smile (think more "Mona Lisa" and less "say cheese!") Hold your gentle smile for a few seconds, and notice how it feels.

I helped make this amazing moment happen

When things do go exactly as you planned, and your child is in good spirits and you share a meaningful experience together, don't just chalk it up to chance. You participated in making it happen. You supported your child with your loving presence and attention. Acknowledge your contribution.

mindful carpool

Like many mothers, you may spend a lot of time driving kids from one activity to the next. If you are playing chauffeur today, see if you can use that time to connect with your child and her friends: talk about their activities, sing together, or play a classic game, such as "I spy."

tender kisses

If you get a kiss from your child today, savor this expression of love. Notice if her kiss is gentle or full of pressure, if it's big or small, if it's loud or quiet. Inhale the sweet smell of her skin and hair. Can you feel or hear her heartbeat? Check in with what it feels like to receive this act of tenderness and care from your child.

when we cling to the good

With mindfulness, we come to realize that all of our difficult moments will ultimately pass. And that means our good moments will eventually come to an end, too. The secret to truly living and loving those moments is to not cling to them. Sometimes we hold those experiences so tightly, fearing they may never come again, that we almost crush them. We don't even really enjoy them because we're so worried that they'll end. They will end, as all moments do. When we don't frantically cling to the good, and relax into it instead, it expands and nourishes us.

✦ ✦ ✦ ✦ ✦ ✦ ✦ ✦ ✦ ✦ ✦ ✦ ✦ ✦ ✦ ✦ ✦ ✦

music meditation

Put on some music you like and pay attention to how you feel as you listen. What do you notice in your body? What thoughts arise? Does the music make you feel calm, energized, or something else? Savor the power music has to awaken so many emotions, memories, thoughts, sensations, and experiences.

CHAPTER 8

CLOSE OF DAY
EVENING PRACTICES

Today you had an invitation—to show up, to make mistakes, to make amends, and to pay attention. Tonight is a time to invite rest and reflection. It is a time to be compassionate with yourself for your mistakes, to commit to new intentions for tomorrow, and to nurture yourself with loving care and restorative sleep. In this chapter, you'll find practices for closing your day with presence, stillness, and love.

bedtime meditation

When my children were infants, rocking them to sleep at night became a meditation. I knew that once their eyes closed, if I counted to 100 they would stay asleep when I put them down in their crib. I would begin counting in time to my rocking, which started to match the rhythm of my breath. Staring at a sweet sleeping face, the numbers in my head became a mantra, tethering me to the present moment and allowing me to savor the end of this day with my child.

✦ ✦ ✦ ✦ ✦ ✦ ✦ ✦ ✦ ✦ ✦ ✦ ✦ ✦ ✦ ✦ ✦

sleeping beauty

Before you go to bed, check in on your sleeping child. Notice how relaxed his face and body are, observe the gentle rise and fall of his chest, and listen to the soft sounds of his breath. Place your hand on your heart and notice how your body feels as you watch your child in sweet repose. This tender image of your sleeping child can be called upon at any moment of your day when you need to remind yourself of the innate goodness and sweetness of your little one.

what moved you today?

Did your four-year-old drop a truth-bomb? Did you get a sweet and unexpected hug from your teen? Did a wave of deep love or empathy swell up and surprise you? Did you witness a kind act between your children, or by a stranger? Did you get a misspelled and grammatically incorrect love note from your first-grader? Did you have a moment of presence and awareness and connection? What moved you today?

I WELCOME, AND SAVOR,

REST.

prepare for tomorrow

You probably have routines for readying the house and the kids for the next morning—selecting outfits, packing lunches, organizing backpacks. Save a few moments to prepare yourself mentally for tomorrow. What will be needed of you? What do you need? Will you be facing a difficult situation? Spend a few moments tonight preparing yourself for your encounter with tomorrow.

bedroom retreat

As it's often the last place you tidy up, take some time today to make your bedroom a nurturing space to retreat to at the end of the day: diffuse some lavender essential oil, light a candle, fluff up your pillows, add a fuzzy blanket to your bed, get a heating pad or hot-water bottle, or just clear out the clutter so you can truly relax at the end of your day.

night sky meditation

Before you go to bed tonight, step outside and look up at the night sky. Whether you see just a few stars or an entire galaxy, take a moment to remind yourself that you are stardust. You and the stars and your kids and all the other mothers are all made from the same shining universe stuff. You're all in this together, and you, yes you, are a star.

sleep as surrender

As you climb into bed tonight, remember that sleep is a powerful lesson in surrender: we don't know when and how we will slide from wakefulness into slumber, but we know it will happen. All we can do is create the proper conditions, and then lie down and trust.

◇ ◇

sleeping beauty

Before you go to bed, check in on your sleeping child. Notice how relaxed his face and body are, observe the gentle rise and fall of his chest, and listen to the soft sounds of his breath. Place your hand on your heart and notice how your body feels as you watch your child in sweet repose.

TODAY WAS HARD. BUT I DID IT. AND I AM STRONGER FOR IT.

your mindful life

With mindfulness, we accept whatever is present. Because that's WHAT IS. It's not resignation—it's simply recognizing this is what it's like right now. And then we have a choice. If it's something we can change, we can work in the next moment to change it. If it's something we cannot change, we can choose to soften into it. Mindfulness doesn't eliminate the stressors from your life. Your children will still throw tantrums, people will still cut you off in traffic, and it may rain sometimes. The profound transformation takes place within you. You choose to relate to the stressors in life more skillfully. And that is LIFE-CHANGING. You've got this, mama.

index

resources

WEBSITES

**Left Brain Buddha:
The Modern Mindful Life**
www.leftbrainbuddha.com
Author's blog.

Mindful Parenting
blogs.psychcentral.com/
mindful-parenting
*Blog by Carla Naumburg, Ph.D.,
at Psych Central.*

Dr Dan Siegel
www.drdansiegel.com
Resources on mindfulness.

Greater Good Science Center
greatergood.berkeley.edu/
mindfulness
Articles and more.

APPS

All the apps listed below are
available for iOS and Android.

For mothers:
Headspace
10% Happier
Insight Timer
Calm

For kids:
Stop, Breathe, & Think
Smiling Mind

Breathe Think Do with Sesame
Settle Your Glitter

BOOKS

*Everyday Blessings: The Inner
Work of Mindful Parenting*
by Myla and Jon Kabat-Zinn,
Hachette, 1998

*The Mindful Child: How to Help
Your Kid Manage Stress and
Become Happier, Kinder, and
More Compassionate*
by Susan Kaiser Greenland,
Atria Books, 2010

Parenting in the Present Moment
by Carla Naumburg, Ph.D, Parallax
Press, 2014

*Ready, Set, Breathe: Practicing
Mindfulness with Your Children for
Fewer Meltdowns and a More
Peaceful Family* by Carla
Naumburg, Ph.D, New Harbinger
Publications, 2015

*The Whole-Brain Child: 12
Revolutionary Strategies to
Nurture Your Child's Developing
Mind* by Daniel J. Siegel, M.D.,
and Tina Payne Bryson, Ph.D.,
Bantam, 2012